Driving Tips for BOOH's (Bats Out Of Hell)

A Satirical & Humorous Instruction Manual

By

E.A. James

FM Publishing Company
Cherokee, NC 28719

Driving Tips for BOOH's (Bats Out Of Hell)
A Satirical & Humorous Instruction Manual

Published by:

FM Publishing Company
P.O. Box 215
Cherokee, NC 28719
United States of America
www.fmpublishingcompany.com

Printed in the United States of America

ISBN 9781931671415

Table of Contents

Introduction

This manual is NOT a real instruction manual. It is intended as humor and satire only. It is also NOT meant to laugh at DUI and DWI drivers. These types of drivers are NOT the same as a BOOH (Bat Out Of Hell).

This manual has two main purposes: (1) to help you understand your role as a true BOOH; and (2) to provide you with a few tips to help maintain your status as a true BOOH.

The information contained in this handbook is not intended to be an official legal reference to any traffic laws. It is intended only to explain, in everyday language, those rules, and driving practices & procedures that a BOOH will use most often. It should be noted that the material in this manual is subject to change.

The three most basic traffic laws require drivers to:

1. Obey traffic control devices (lights and signs);

2. Obey the traffic directions of a law enforcement officer or firefighter, even if it goes against what the traffic control devices tell you to do;

3. Never drive on a roadway that has been closed for construction, for the purpose of a special event, or for any other official reason.

So here's the good news for BOOH's: since everyone else is obeying the traffic laws, this leaves your options wide open! While they're obeying the rules, you have free reign.

BOOH Who?

Whenever a BOOH gets behind a wheel
Only another BOOH can imagine the thrill
Fast and furious to reach their own destination
Without regard for others and without hesitation

They'll pass before you know it and even change lanes
Stopping only for pedestrians and maybe for trains
Their intention is not to harm, but don't get in their way
"There goes another Bat Out Of Hell," is all we can say

Tip #1: You Don't Have to Worry About Laws Governing Right-of-Way

According to most State driving laws, right-of-way "is a phrase used to describe who has the lawful authority to enter a roadway, change lanes within a roadway, make a turn from a roadway, travel through an intersection, or make any other traffic related movement."

These laws further state that "vehicle drivers (including bicyclists) and pedestrians should always understand the rules related to right-of-way, and remember that right-of-way is something to be given, not taken. There may be instances in which you as a driver or pedestrian have the legal right-of-way over someone else, even though the other person does not realize it and is not obeying the rules of the road. In those instances, the right-of-way should be yielded in order to prevent a crash."

How's that for good news? Good drivers will never take the right of way; they will yield to you, the BOOH. They will yield to you to avoid a crash. Therefore, drive like you always do. However, a BOOH does not run over pedestrians. They realize their loveable and expensive car is dangerous to people who are on foot. Remember, you're a free spirit not a killer.

Tip #2: What to Do In Specific Right-of-Way Situations

On a Roadway

When traveling on a roadway that intersects with another roadway, if you are faced with a stop sign, but other traffic is not, A BOOH will always proceed without stopping.

At intersections with no stop signs, yield signs, or other traffic signals.

The law says that if two vehicles come to the intersection at the same time, the driver of the vehicle on the left must yield to the driver of the vehicle on the right. You, as a BOOH, do not have time to figure out if you arrived at the same time or which side you are on. It is always assumed you are in the right. In such cases, a BOOH will always proceed.

At a four-way intersection where all drivers are faced with stop signs

As a BOOH, you will always yield to pedestrians; however, once the pedestrian has crossed, a BOOH will pay no attention to the "first to arrive, first to proceed" order. You will proceed as if in an intersection with no stop signs, yield signals, or other traffic signals.

When making a left turn at an intersection, or into an alley or driveway

All traffic coming from the opposite direction must yield to the BOOH because you are not about to stop. You must keep on the move. It's is already an imposition to have to wait a long, horrendous 90 seconds for a red light to change and/or get a green arrow. In cases like this, you have to keep moving.

When approaching a yield sign

When you approach a yield sign, the other drivers should slow down to a safe speed and be prepared to stop because you are not about to. If necessary, the other drivers should stop and only proceed after you are out of sight.

When the roadway you are traveling on is merging into other traffic without stopping

In this case the other drivers behind you should adjust their speed and vehicle position to allow you to merge into the new lane safely. Traffic from another roadway that is merging into the roadway you are traveling on should quickly and safely change lanes away from you, if possible. If it is not possible to change lanes away from you, they need to adjust their speed and vehicle position to safely allow the BOOH to merge into the traffic.

At intersections with traffic control lights

Try your best to speedily make it through, especially if the light has been red for a second or two. Good drivers have been warned to make sure they wait until the intersection is clear of traffic or approaching traffic before entering and not to proceed "just because" they have the green light. So, you have plenty of time.

Entering or crossing a highway from an alley, private road or highway

Make sure you stop and yield the right-of-way to all pedestrians. However, if vehicles are already traveling on the roadway or sidewalk you are entering or crossing, quickly and repeatedly blaring your horn so they know you are coming through.

Uniformed Fun Stopper (UFS), fire, or ambulance service vehicles are using their emergency lights (blue or red) and sirens

Quickly put on your emergency shades and earphones. This is the time to turn up your music because those sirens can be deafening to the ear drums. Remember, a BOOH's vehicle can travel just as fast as emergency vehicles, or the Uniformed Fun Stopper (UFS) (or "police" to everyone else). So, be sure to speed up when you hear or see them coming. Chances are the UFS's are on a call so they won't bother about you. Once again, however, make sure there is no one on a bicycle or a pedestrian is in the way at the time.

Highway maintenance vehicles and workers in a construction zone

Avoid at all costs. Usually, a true BOOH will never be caught in these areas.

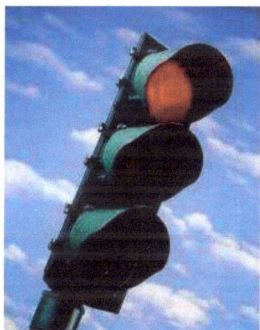

Right turn on red light

Duh! Even good drivers know that unless a sign posted at that intersection prohibits doing so, it is permissible to make a "right turn on red" at an intersection controlled by a traffic control light. They may proceed only after making a complete stop, yielding to all traffic, BOOH's and pedestrians, and making the determination that they can safely complete the turn. BOOH's are going to make the turn regardless.

Left turn on red light

Again, good drivers know that unless a sign posted at an that intersection prohibits doing so, it is permissible to make a "left turn on red" from the left lane of a one-way street onto a one-way street on which the traffic moves toward the driver's left. Of course, they may proceed only after making a complete stop, yielding to BOOH's and stopping for pedestrians, and making the determination that they can safely complete the turn. You, on the other hand, may proceed at all times.

When a school bus is preparing to stop to load or unload children

This one is without compromise for even true BOOH's. You will see the driver of the bus activating flashing yellow lights. When seeing these flashing yellow lights, all vehicles approaching the school bus should slow down and be prepared to stop. All drivers should pay special attention to children who may be walking along or crossing the roadway. Once the flashing lights have turned red and the stop signs have extended from the side of the bus, it is unlawful for any vehicle to pass the stopped school bus while it is loading or unloading passengers. On a highway divided by a median, cars traveling on the opposite side from the stopped school bus are not required to stop, however drivers should remain attentive for children walking along or crossing the roadway. Of course, as a rule, BOOH's try to avoid school zones. If unavoidable, BOOH's will stop and mutter how come the "little twerps" are still in school and haven't gotten jobs yet.

NOTE: In the State of Georgia, there is what is called a "Move Over Law." This states that when an emergency vehicle with flashing lights is parked on the shoulder of the highway, drivers are to move over one lane, slow down, or be prepared to stop, if they have to. As a BOOH, you will automatically move over anyway without signaling the other drivers, but at no time will a BOOH slow down or stop. True BOOH's will always plan ahead for these situations. In most cases, they try not to drive in Georgia.

Which brings us to Tip #3 . . .

Tip #3: How to Pass Other Vehicles Like You Pass Gas

On A Two-Lane Road

A passing zone is indicated by striped lines to the right of the center line of the roadway. If the line nearest to your vehicle is solid, you know you are not in a passing zone, but you don't care. As a true BOOH, you know how to look ahead along the roadway to determine the length of the passing zone and if there is traffic approaching from the opposite direction. Also, as a BOOH, you always think you have sufficient time and space to execute your passing maneuver and return your vehicle completely to the right lane before the passing zone ends, before entering an intersection, and before oncoming traffic is just inches away from your vehicle.

You are an expert at checking your rear view and side mirrors for "blind spots" to make sure that no one is passing you. Not only wouldn't they dare pass a BOOH, but you are traveling much too fast for them to do so. In most cases, you are their "blind spot."

Never, ever give your left turn signal as you begin passing. A signal only signals the other driver what you are doing and ensures that they will try to speed up before you can get over. Besides, we know that BOOH's are free spirits and will never let anyone know what their plans are, especially on the road.

Also, since other drivers will not be passing from the right as the law recommends, you have another available option. You, of course, can pass from the left or the right, whatever meets your needs at the time.

Illegal Signal

The State of Georgia has one law with which BOOH's agree 100%. Drivers should never flash their turn signal to let other drivers behind them know it is ok to pass. BOOH's do not need their signals or their permission and will pass anyway.

Stopped Cars & Pedestrians

Of course, when there are stopped cars allowing for a pedestrian, BOOH's will give way to their little selfish desires and yield, and sometimes even stop,

Passing Bicyclists

The law says that bicyclists have the same rights and responsibilities on the road as motorists. Bicyclists are permitted to travel in the center of the traffic lane if there are safety hazards on the right side of the road (such as parked cars or debris) or if the lane is too narrow for a bicycle and a vehicle to share. This is where it gets tricky for BOOH'S. Since bicyclists want to be treated as any other vehicle, a true BOOH will surely accommodate them!

Passing Motorcyclists

A motorcyclist legally occupies the full width of a single lane when traveling. The law says that when passing a motorcyclist, a driver must pass in an adjacent lane and that drivers are not permitted to occupy the same lane as a motorcyclist while passing them. As a true BOOH, you care nothing for which lane you are in. In fact, you are often on a motorcycle. This is your high time as a BOOH and when other drivers should surely beware.

Weaving

As a BOOH you are constantly weaving in and out of traffic to speed up the flow of traffic. And, of course, you never give a signal for reasons stated earlier.

Tip #4: Making Turns: Driving Others Crazy with the Least Amount of Effort

Making Right & Left Turns

Good drivers will be using appropriate signals, and giving drivers ahead of and behind them adequate notice to indicate a right or left turn. They will be approaching the intersection in the right or left lane and staying as close as possible to the curb or edge of the roadway.

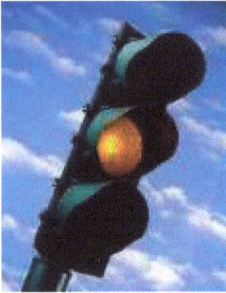

Now they, like a BOOH, will be watching out for bicyclists and yielding to those who are traveling straight through the intersection before they make a right or left turn.

However, they, unlike you, will be making their turn in such a way as to end up in the right lane (if making a right turn) or the left lane (if making a left turn) of the street into which they have turned and avoid entering any other lane of traffic. Also, if there are multiple turning lanes on the street from which they are turning, they will complete the turn so that their vehicle ends up in the corresponding lane on the street onto which they are turning.

You, on the other hand, will be turning into whatever lane is available, making sure to make full use of the lane of traffic in the opposing direction if it is not currently occupied by other cars. However, once again, everyone, including BOOH's will be making sure to give the right of way to pedestrians at all times, especially when making a right or left turn.

Making U-Turns

BOOH's will turn anywhere at any time. They are never limited and always reserve the right to change their mind in mid-stream. A U-turn allows for this flexibility in plans, whether a sign is posted prohibiting this type of turn or not.

Making Turns on Multi-Lane Highways

On a multi-lane, two-way highway, good drivers never drive to the left of the center line except when making a left turn. If traffic control signals or signs are present, these drivers will usually only complete the turn when authorized to do so by the traffic control signals or signs. As usual, when making left turns, they always yield to oncoming traffic, and wait for pedestrians to clear the lanes of traffic, driveway, sidewalk, or alley you are turning into.

A BOOH will drive to the left, right, middle, on top of other cars, wherever their spirits lead them, but will yield to pedestrians and pedestrians only.

Tip #5: Making Expert Car Maneuvers

Stopping, Standing, or Parking

BOOH's will ignore any all rules pertaining to those prohibiting stopping, standing, or parking, because they realize that any driver who has to stop, stand, or park near or on highways, bridges, intersections, crosswalks, fire hydrants, overpasses, subways, railroad stations, excavation or construction sites, stop signs, or signals are born losers! Therefore, no one should look for a BOOH to provide assistance. A BOOH surely does not have the time.

Parallel Parking

No one should ever force BOOH's to parallel park. Most of the time, BOOH's will beat you to a space where you have been waiting to park; however, if BOOH's are forced to parallel park and no one is around, they will get into the space the best way possible. Sometimes this means they will have to double park. BOOH's give the term "double parking" a whole new meaning. For them, this means on top of your car. If they have to fit into the space, minimal damage to the car in front of them and the car behind them is optional. This brings us to the next maneuver.

Backing Up

Before backing, a BOOH will never check all sides of their vehicle to make sure it is safe to do so. A BOOH will never turn their head and look over their right shoulder while backing; they will depend solely on their mirrors. If a BOOH (God forbid) has duped someone into giving them a job as a driver of a bus or big rig, the BOOH will not use all mirrors and, as a free and independent spirit, will never utilize another person to observe and direct them while backing the vehicle. This would give someone else too much control, and for a BOOH, this cannot happen.

Tip #6: Taking Credit for Enacted Speeding Laws

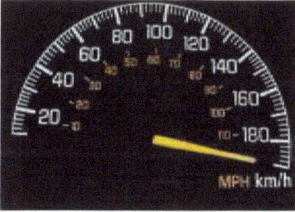

Super Speeder

All BOOH's should take a big bow. It was because of your repeated disregard for safe driving laws that on July 1, 2009 the new Georgia Super Speeder law came into effect. Now, any driver convicted of speeding 75 mph on any two-lane road, or 85 mph and over anywhere in Georgia, will be fined a $200 state fee. The new state fees will be in addition to any local fines already in effect in the jurisdiction where the speeding offense occurs. As a BOOH, you should be proud.

Speed Limits

BOOH's are highly intelligent and make it their business to be aware of rules – before they break them. Although most BOOH's try their best to stay out of Georgia, there are, however, many who do either reside there or choose to visit family members who live there. So, below are the maximum traveling speeds in Georgia unless otherwise posted:

- 30 miles per hour in any urban or residential district
- 35 miles per hour on an unpaved county road
- 70 miles per hour on a rural interstate
- 65 miles per hour on an urban interstate or on a multi-lane divided highway
- 55 miles per hour in all other areas

It is understood that the average speed for a BOOH is at least 60 miles per hour when no UFS is around.

Driving Too Slowly

Ha-ha, ha-ha, ha-ha! Not a chance!

Tip #7: Getting Through Railroads and Work Zones

Railroad Crossings

A BOOH will only stop (and more than likely it won't be within 50 feet) in the following instances:

- A train is blocking the crossing
- A man waving a flag is blocking the crossing and there is no way around him
- An animal is blocking the crossing and it's not the type of meat that a BOOH likes to eat.
- A UFS is in close proximity
- The BOOH happens to be in a car other than their Hummer and would damage the car by smashing through the crossing gate

Work Zones

When BOOH's travel through a work zone they will:

1. Never reduce their speed.

2. Hardly ever adjust their lane position away from workers.

3. Always prepare for the unexpected!

4. Watch for UFS's because fines are increased in most work zones.

5. Almost always coast whenever possible, especially when traveling downhill.

Tip #8: Knowing and Adhering to the Few BOOH-Approved Laws

Though they be few and far in between, BOOH's do have some rules they agree with absolutely 100%.

Driving Under the Influence of Drugs or Alcohol

Never at anytime will a BOOH waste their time by operating a vehicle while under the influence of alcohol, a drug, or any other substance which will impair their ability to do so. A BOOH must have full use of their faculties when they cause another vehicle to be run off the road.

Reckless Driving

Time and time again, BOOH's have received a bad rap for reckless driving. The law says that reckless driving is "driving any vehicle in reckless disregard for the safety of persons or property," and that "penalties for reckless driving can include a fine of up to $1000, imprisonment for up to 12 months, and, if the driver is under 21 years of age, conviction will result in a suspension of all driving privileges." BOOH's are expert drivers; they know it and everyone else should know it. Except for railroad crossing signs and certain animals, BOOH's almost never harm anyone. They make it a point to cause accidents, not get involved in them.

Racing

A BOOH will never be involved in racing. Here's why. The law describes racing behavior in these terms:

1. When two or more people compete or race on any street or highway. First of all, BOOH's consider themselves without competition. You can't catch them.

2. When one motor vehicle is beside or to the rear of another driver, and one driver tries to prevent the passing or overtaking of the competing driver by acceleration or maneuver. A BOOH won't try to stop others from passing them. Chances are they're not traveling fast enough to do so anyway.

3. When one or more persons compete in a race against time. BOOH's have better things to do than engage in such childish behavior. They are in their own race against time at all times and it's not with other drivers. Hopefully, no one takes it personally. However, as a true BOOH, you really don't care. You just keep moving.

Aggressive Driving

The laws states that aggressive driving occurs when a person "operates any motor vehicle with the intent to annoy, harass, molest, intimidate, injure, or obstruct another person." Let it be known here and now that BOOH's never drive with the intent to do any of these things. These are just the results of being a BOOH. As stated earlier, a BOOH is not involved in accidents; they just cause them; however, it is never premeditated. This involves caring about the existence of others, which is not a consistent characteristic of a true BOOH.

Obstructing the Driver's View

All BOOH's wholeheartedly agree that a vehicle which is overloaded with passengers or freight in such a way that they obstruct the   driver's view or interfere with the mechanical operation, should not be allowed on the road. As a BOOH, you want to ensure that such drivers do not get in your way.

Following Emergency Vehicles

BOOH's already drive like they're in emergency vehicles, minus the sirens and flashing lights. They know that if an emergency vehicle is responding to a fire alarm or some other emergency, a UFS is likely to be in vicinity. In such cases, a BOOH will always steer clear.

Littering the Highways

BOOH's understand that, according to most State laws, the term "litter" refers to "all sand, gravel, slag, brick bats, rubbish, waste material, tin cans, refuse, garbage, trash, dead animals or discarded materials of every kind and description." As a result of being a BOOH, there is possibly a litter of vehicles, animals, or vehicles containing such items described above, as a direct result of a BOOH having caused maybe one, two, three, possibly even ten accidents. However, a BOOH will never intentionally discard rubbish or trash on the highways. Remember, as a BOOH, you really don't have the time to do so.

Caravanning

BOOH's are independent and considered loners. They will never be part of a caravan. In addition, they are unequivocally opposed to trailers over 8 feet or huge vehicles that get in their way and can possibly prevent them from overtaking and passing them or occupying a space on the road. According to BOOH's, this practice should be outlawed.

Riding in Trailers

Are you kidding? Not ever, ever, ever!

Tip #9: Remembering You Were Born To Be Wild

Median Strip

BOOH's consider a dividing section, barrier, or unpaved strip which separates two roadways at any point as another point of access to get where they need to go. They know that the shortest distance between any two points is a straight line.

Impaired Hearing and Vision

BOOH's use headsets, headphones, or eye shades only as needed as described earlier: when the sound of a siren or lights of an emergency vehicle is deafening or blinding to a BOOH's internal, free spirit.

Opening Vehicle Doors

A BOOH will only do this when they are being chased by a UFS and have a need to jump out.

One Way Streets

A BOOH will only travel in the opposite direction that a street is supposed to go when it is absolutely necessary. Most of the times a BOOH feels it is absolutely necessary. Let others hinder themselves in this fashion. A BOOH will not. However, a BOOH is an expert driver, and will watch out for pedestrians and pedestrians only. Others need to take precautions and drive defensively. A BOOH always expects others to do so.

Stopping

A BOOH will stop or slow down without notice. You will see no hand or arm signal, nor will they use a brake operated stop signal. As stated earlier, a BOOH will not let others in on their plans.

Using Headlights

BOOH's will make full use of their high-beam headlights whenever necessary. To BOOH's, dimming their headlights at night is like dimming their free spirits. They must shine their lights at all times. If you get blinded in the meantime, just know that it has nothing to do with trying to harm you; it has everything to do with the fact that BOOH's care only about themselves and reaching their destination.

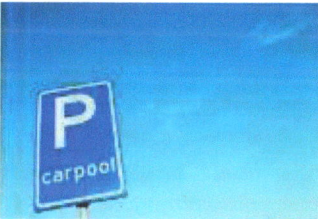

The Right Not To Carpool

BOOH's care nothing about the ozone layer or air pollution due to carbon monoxide. They also don't care about vehicle emissions. BOOH's make it a point to drive cars that run fast and efficiently. If there is a problem, they get another car or truck. And never should anyone ask a BOOH to carpool or think to sell this point by mentioning how this would help the air quality. BOOH's are loners who must have full use of their vehicle whenever they need it. Don't anyone ask a BOOH to pick them up or give them a ride. To a BOOH, this person will be considered dead weight because it would surely slow them down, and this can never happen.

Tip #10: If It Looks Like a Duck And Quacks Like a Duck, Call It a Duck

To a BOOH, one of the most ridiculous of all laws is the one against idling engines. A BOOH considers this a complete oxymoron, much like:

- Authentic replica
- Business casual
- Close distance
- Dim light
- Express mail
- Friendly divorce
- Government worker
- Head butt
- Insane logic
- Justice Rehnquist
- Kosher ham
- Limited freedom
- Mild PMS
- Normal deviation
- One choice
- Pretty ugly
- Quiet storm
- Rush hour
- Speed limit
- Taliban intelligence
- Unbiased opinion
- Voluntary taxes
- Waiting patiently
- Young adult
- Zero deficit

Important Final Reminders for BOOH's

So, there you have it from A to Z. This last section gives a few final reminders for true BOOH's:

1. Never, at any time, do you signal. This would be too considerate and courteous and would let other drivers know what you are planning to do. You, as a BOOH, do not want anyone in on your plans for the future, especially while on the road.

2. Drive in one lane ONLY if it is absolutely necessary! BOOH's must maintain their spontaneity at all times and must keep their options open. You should not allow restrictions or silly things like rules of the road to become a hindrance to your freedom of expression.

3. Never mind what your State has classified on your driver's license; you are not a Class A, B, C, or D. BOOH's are in a class all by themselves. You are the exception to every rule.

4. Always remember that driving is a responsibility that carries many privileges. Please continue to be a true and dependable BOOH at all times.

About The Author

Dr. Elizabeth A. James (E.A. James) has been writing for over 40 years. She is a licensed and ordained minister and has been President and Founder of Fast And Indispensable Temporary Help (F.A.I.T.H.) Ministries, Inc. since February, 1999. She is also the Editor-in-Chief of FM Publishing Company (2009) and Senior Managing Director of Geri Lorraine Enterprises, LLC (2000). In 2014, she became a supplier, independent marketer, and supporter with TAG Team Marketing International and a dedicated member of the Black Business Network.

After attending over 10 colleges, she has a doctorate in Theology & Biblical Counseling, a master's in Education, bachelor's degree in English, and major course work in subjects such as Business Management, Biomedical Engineering, Pre-Med, and Chemistry.

In addition to many other accomplishments, E.A. James has received the Woman of Excellence Award, is a member of blackwritersconnect.com, and has won several awards for her poetry. She is currently a business consultant, certified teacher, and a Nationally-Certified Manager of Program Improvement.

Titles by E.A. James:

Spiritual Cosmetics for the Soul (devotionals)
The Last Visitor (historical fiction)
Being a Well Body of Believers (nonfiction)
This Hill I Climb (poetry)
The Reason Why I Sing (poetry/songs)
Driving Tips for BOOHs (Bats Out of Hell) (satire)
7-Day Emergency Help for OWIACs (Of Whom I Am Chief) (devotionals)
Why I Should Hate Men, But Don't (nonfiction)
Will Work for Food, Family & Freedom (nonfiction)
Casino Con: An Eye-Opening Look From the Inside Out (nonfiction)

Book Ordering Information

To order other books by E.A. James or books published by FM Publishing Company, or to inquire about screenplay production rights, go to:

www.fmpublishingcompany.com

www.blackbusinessnetwork.com/doctorlj

www.createspace.com

www.amazon.com

www.lightningsource.com

Email: fmpublishing@cox.net

Fax: 800-518-1219

www.ingramcontent.com/pod-product-compliance
Lightning Source LLC
Chambersburg PA
CBHW041807040426
42448CB00005B/301